# THE
# ROMAN
# COLOSSEUM

**Series Editor** David Salariya
**Book Editor** Penny Clarke

**Author:**
**Fiona Macdonald** studied history at Cambridge University and the University of East Anglia, where she is a part-time Tutor in Medieval History. She has also taught in schools and adult education, and is the author of numerous books for children on historical topics, including *Roman Fort*, *Viking Town* and *Medieval Castle* in the award-winning **Inside Story** series.

**Illustrator:**
**Mark Bergin** was born in Hastings in 1961. He studied at Eastbourne College of Art and has specialized in historical reconstruction since leaving art school in 1983. He lives with his wife and family in East Sussex.

© The Salariya Book Co Ltd MCMXCVI

Created, designed and produced by
The Salariya Book Co Ltd, Brighton, UK.

Published by
PETER BEDRICK BOOKS
2112 Broadway
New York, NY 10023

Published by agreement with Macdonald Young Books Ltd, England

Library of Congress Cataloging-in-Publication Data
Macdonald, Fiona.
    The Roman Colosseum / Fiona Macdonald, Mark Bergin.
      p. cm. – (Inside story)
    Includes index.
    Summary: An illustrated survey of the construction and history of the Colosseum, the enormous oval amphitheater that has stood in Rome for 1,900 years.
    ISBN 0-87226-275-8
    1. Colosseum (Rome, Italy) – Juvenile literature.
2. Amphitheaters – Rome – Juvenile literature. 3. Rome (Italy) –
– Buildings, structures, etc. – Juvenile literatures. 4. Rome
(Italy) – Antiquities – Pictorial works – Juvenile literature.
[1. Colosseum (Rome, Italy) 2. Rome (Italy) – Antiquities.]
I. Bergin, Mark. II. Title. III. Series: Inside story (Peter
Bedrick Books)
DG68. 1. M24' 1996                            96-15138
937'.8 – dc20                                        CIP
                                                          AC

Printed in Hong Kong

00 99 98 97 96 1 2 3 4 5

# THE
# ROMAN
# COLOSSEUM

FIONA MACDONALD · MARK BERGIN

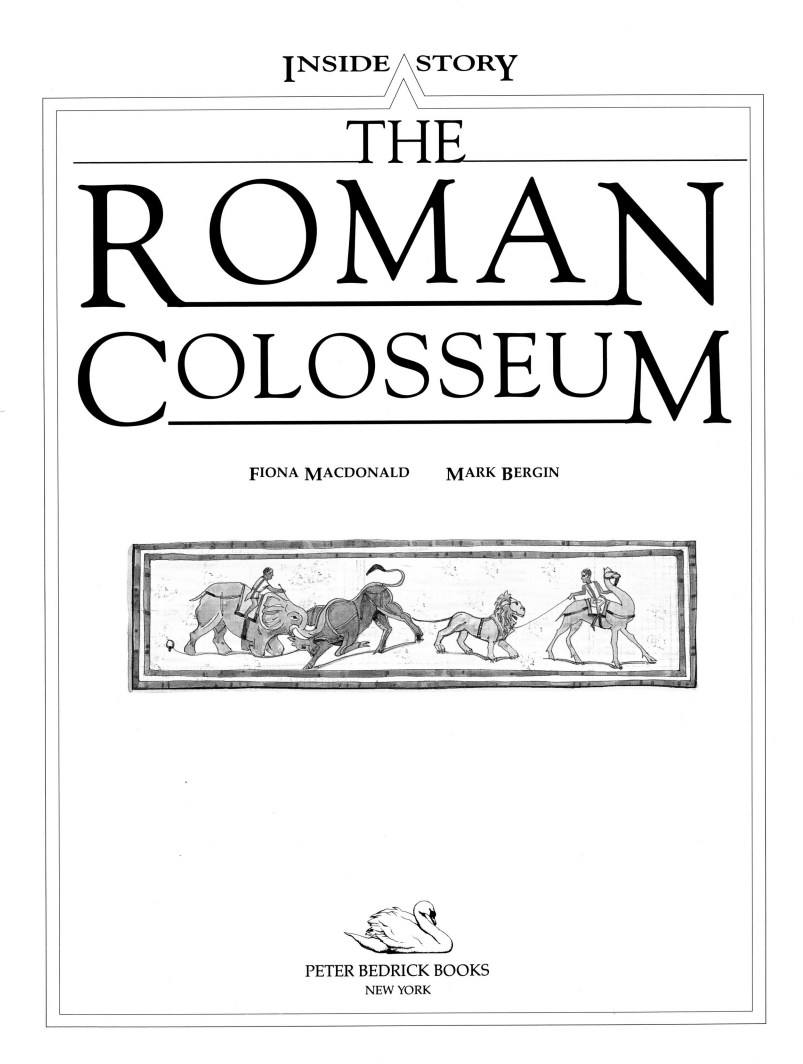

PETER BEDRICK BOOKS

NEW YORK

# CONTENTS

# INTRODUCTION

The enormous oval-shaped amphitheater known as the Colosseum has stood close to the middle of Rome for 1,900 years. Ever since it was first completed, in AD 96, people have admired its vast size and bold design. It measures 187 feet high, 617 feet across (at its widest point) and 1,729 feet – about a third of a mile – round the outside. Many legends have grown up about it, the most famous being that if the Colosseum is ever destroyed, then the city of Rome will also be destroyed.

Throughout the ages, the Colosseum has been admired as a magnificent building, and an impressive feat of engineering. But today most people would find little to admire in the 'entertainments' that were staged in it: the thousands of gladiators, captives and criminals who died fighting in the Colosseum, or the millions of animals that were slaughtered in the Colosseum's wild-beast shows to satisfy the spectators' lust for blood. They also remember the hundreds of brave Christian men and women who were killed because of their beliefs.

But to the ancient Romans, the Colosseum was a noble monument to a powerful ruling family, a popular place of entertainment and a sacred arena where 'holy and ancient games' (as one Roman writer described them) were staged.

# THE ROMAN WORLD

The eagle was the symbol of the Roman empire.

The Colosseum was built during the first century AD, when the Roman empire was growing ever richer and more powerful. Roman governors, backed up by Roman armies, ruled over conquered territories and administered Roman laws. Roman tax collectors sent money levied from conquered peoples back to the emperors' treasury in Rome. Roman merchants went all over the empire, buying valuable goods to sell to rich citizens in Rome.

**The Roman empire** at its largest and most powerful, around AD 100. The empire stretched from Scotland to the Middle East.

Corn, wine, honey, olive oil and spices came from the empire's farms. Valuable raw materials, such as marble, metal and wool, and luxury goods like silk, papyrus, glass, furs and jewels were seized by soldiers, paid as tribute, or purchased by wealthy citizens.

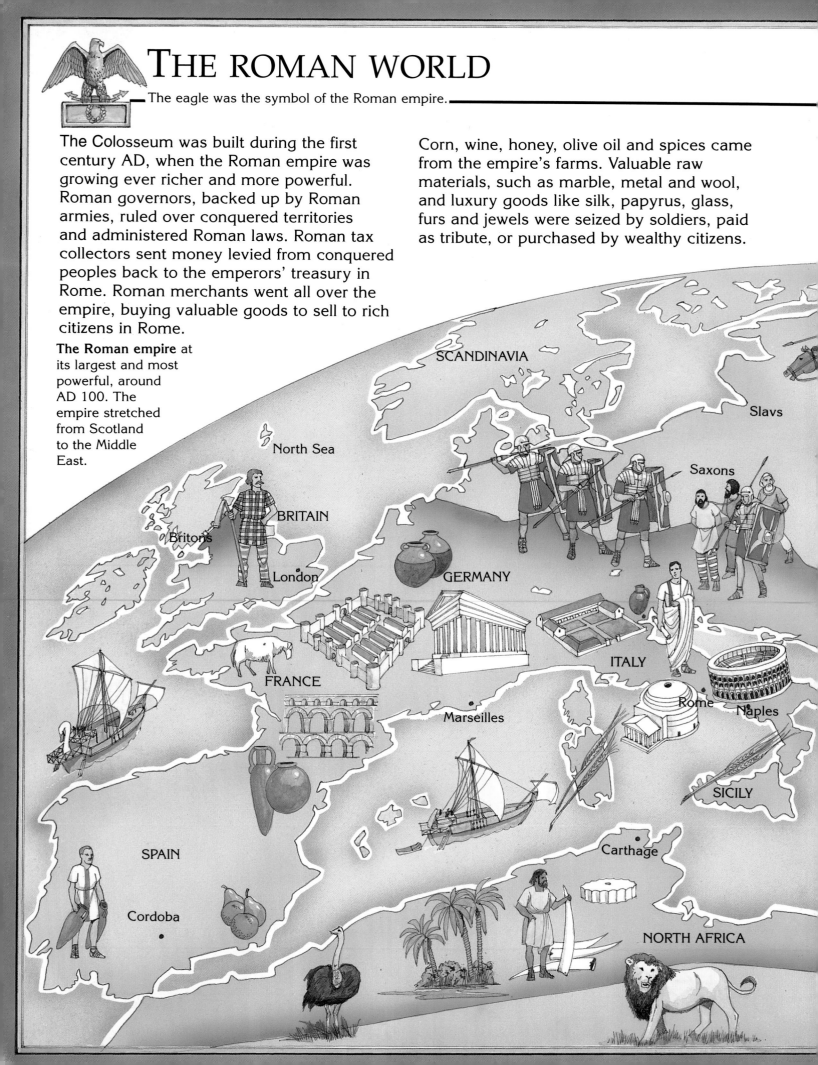

SCANDINAVIA

Slavs

North Sea

Saxons

BRITAIN

Britons

London

GERMANY

ITALY

FRANCE

Rome    Naples

Marseilles

SICILY

Carthage

SPAIN

Cordoba

NORTH AFRICA

In Roman times, the countries of present-day Europe did not exist. Instead, the land was occupied by many warring tribes. By AD 100, the Romans had conquered most of these tribes. Only the northern Germans, the Scandinavians and Slavs remained free.

The Roman empire reached its greatest size during the reign of Emperor Trajan (AD 98-116). But it stayed at this peak of power and prosperity for less than 100 years. By around AD 200, its authority was declining and conquered peoples were preparing to rebel. The empire finally collapsed in AD 476. But the Colosseum, like many other magnificent Roman buildings, remained standing for future generations to see.

**The greatest threat** to the might of the Roman empire came from wild tribes, like the Huns and Goths, who lived on its north-eastern frontiers.

ASIA

Black Sea

Caspian Sea

MIDDLE EAST

GREECE

Athens

Corinth

Mediterranean Sea

EGYPT

Alexandria

# CITY AND PEOPLE

'Rome, goddess of peoples and continents, nothing can equal you, and nowhere can approach your power.' That was what the Roman poet Martial wrote around AD 80. The heart of the Roman empire, Rome spread over the famous 'Seven Hills', the legendary home of the city's first inhabitants. People arriving in Rome from distant lands were astonished by the riches and beauty of the central districts of the city. They gazed in wonder at the majestic temples and the fine statues of heroes, goddesses and gods. They admired the extravagantly decorated palaces and beautiful gardens belonging to wealthy noble families and the dignified, spacious public buildings built by earlier rulers of Rome.

They strolled, dazzled, through the great Forum – a market-place where merchants sold goods from all over the known world. They stared with respect at a noble senator, carried shoulder-high by slaves in a curtained litter, on his way to a meeting to decide the fate of nations. They joined the noisy, excited crowds watching – and betting on – chariot races at the Circus Maximus. Tired and dirty, they looked longingly at the cheap and relaxing public baths.

## Important buildings in Rome:

1. Theater of Marcellus AD 13.

2. Temple of Emperor Trajan AD 98-117.

3. Trajan's Forum (a huge shopping mall with office blocks above) AD 113.

4. Temple of Jupiter Capitolinus (the city of Rome's own god) c.500 BC and restored many times.

5. Temple of Mars (the god of war) 2 BC.

6. Basilica (building for public meetings and administration) begun by Julius Caesar 49-44 BC, completed by Augustus 30 BC-AD 14.

7. Basilica built by Emperor Maxentius AD 307-313.

8. Temple of Venus (goddess of love) and Roma (goddess of the city of Rome) c.10 BC.

9. Temple of Jupiter (the Romans' most powerful god) 30 BC-AD 14.

10. The Colosseum AD 72-96.

11. Circus Maximus (huge race-track for chariot races) begun 329 BC, rebuilt many times.

12. Aqueduct built by Emperor Nero AD 54-68.

13. Temple of Emperor Claudius AD 41-54.

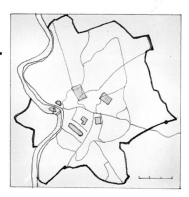

**The city of Rome** was surrounded by walls, strongly rebuilt during the reign of Emperor Aurelian (AD 270-275). Inside the walls were splendid public builings, fine houses, statues and other monuments. Outside the walls were the suburbs where ordinary people lived.

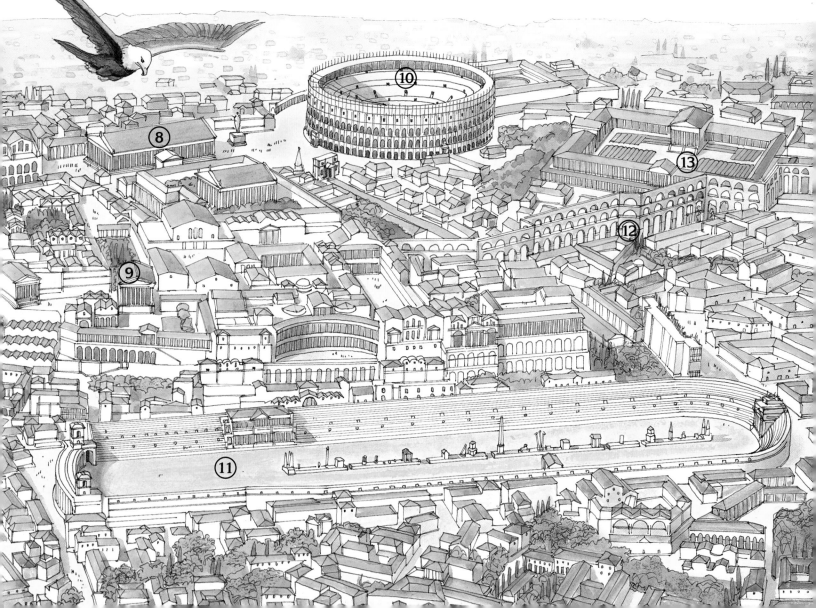

# THE RULING CLASS

For nearly five centuries (509 to 27 BC), Rome was a republic. The government was run by elected officials, who ruled on behalf of the Roman people. In 27 BC, after years of civil war, the old republican system of government was swept away and emperors started to rule Rome. Officially, the emperor's title was 'princeps' (first citizen) but, by the time the Colosseum was being built, Emperor Domitian (ruled AD 81-96) was demanding to be hailed as 'Master and God'.

Like other emperors, Domitian claimed to be more than just a man. Past emperors were worshiped in temples built in their honor after they were dead. Domitian's proud title reveals the emperors' tremendous powers. Massive building projects, like the Colosseum, reveal their vast wealth.

Emperors were expected to rule with the advice of the Senate: an assembly of nobles who had all held senior government posts. The Senate could discuss government policies and pass resolutions (called 'senatus consulta') which had the force of law.

**A member** of the elite Praetorian Guard (top left), one of the most prestigious regiments within the Roman army. During the 2nd century AD, the Praetorian Guard played an important role in government. The members chose, and assassinated, several emperors.

**A patrician** (nobleman) making a speech in the Senate (assembly). Under the Republican system, the Senate was the chief governing body of Rome. Its members discussed (and often shaped) government policy and proposed new laws. Senators all came from patrician (noble) families; they had all held senior government posts. After the Republic ended in 27 BC, the number of senators was reduced, but the Senate still debated emperors' actions and offered advice.

**Although the rich** and noble enjoyed many privileges, plenty of ordinary Roman citizens did too. Citizens could vote and they enjoyed civil rights that the poor, foreigners and slaves did not.

A patrician (noble) family (left). Patricians were rich and influential. Their wealth came from inherited property. Most patrician families owned vast estates in the country which were worked by slaves.

Many patrician families also owned splendid houses and gardens in the city of Rome, with large rooms full of fine furniture.

Many emperors chose to ignore the Senate and follow the advice of palace servants, family and friends. If this advice was good, and the emperor was wise, then Rome and its empire might be well-governed. But if the advice was bad, then problems lay ahead.

# ORDINARY CITIZENS

We do not know the exact population of Rome during the time the Colosseum was being built (AD 72-96), but historians estimate that it was around one million in AD 100. A few noble Roman families were as rich and sophisticated as the city itself. Many more were ordinary, hard-working tradesmen and women, busy in occupations ranging from pastry-makers and perfumers to corn-merchants, silk-weavers and cooks. Other poorer citizens survived on part-time work and state charity. But they were all proud to belong to the city of Rome.

Many of Rome's inhabitants were not official citizens. Roman law allowed peoples from all over the empire to come to Rome, though they did not have full citizen's rights. There was also an enormous population of male and female slaves – around 400,000 in AD 100.

Foreigners and (especially) slaves were governed by harsh laws. For example, a master or mistress could put their slaves to death. But, increasingly, these laws came to matter less and differences in work and wealth between citizens, foreigners and slaves came to matter more. Many foreigners and slaves found good jobs and prospered, while Roman-born citizens remained poor.

**An apartment building,** called an 'insula' ('island'), built in the 1st century AD to provide homes for the rapidly increasing population of Rome. City land was becoming expensive, so Roman engineers designed buildings several stories high to make maximum use of space. Whole families lived in one or two rooms. Water came from the public fountain and there might be a toilet in the courtyard.

extra rooms on roof

**Blocks** of apartments had shops and offices at street level and cramped, drafty attic rooms under the roof. The biggest and best rooms were on the second floor.

flat roof used for storage

**A busy Roman street** in a district where ordinary people lived. In the summer people liked to spend time out of doors away from their small, cramped homes. Many streets were lined with shops and stalls. There were taverns selling hot food and wine, and public toilets and water-fountains on many street corners.

litter

shops

street

# CITY LIFE

Around AD 117, the Roman poet Juvenal wrote, 'How much happier it is to be a rich man's slave than a free-born citizen.' Though they remained proud of their free-born Roman status, the ordinary citizens of Rome had been feeling dissatisfied for years.

One major complaint was about living conditions. Away from the grand central part of the city the streets of Rome were noisy, smelly and dirty. Houses and apartments were ramshackle and crowded. People lived in fear of muggers, burglars and fires.

Another complaint concerned the enormous wealth and power of the few rich families and their slaves. Many slaves were well-trained: they worked as doctors, scribes and accountants. Roman law allowed masters and mistresses to free their slaves (who could then earn high salaries), or leave them large sums of money in their wills. Successful, wealthy slaves and ex-slaves were resented by many ordinary Romans.

But the most serious complaint was about food. So many people lived in the city that wages were low and food prices high. Supplies were unpredictable, too. Around half the people (about 150,000 families in AD 100) could not earn enough to buy food for their families. They relied on free grain from the government to avoid starvation.

**When harvests** failed and grain supplies ran short, as they did in AD 6, the citizens who relied on free food from the state rioted outside government buildings.

**Wheat and barley** to make bread to feed Rome's citizens were carried by ship from the fertile farmlands of Egypt, the vast plains of eastern Europe and the shores of the Black Sea – all part of the Roman empire. Olive oil, wine and fruit were also imported. All these foods were brought to Ostia, Rome's port, about 12 miles from the city.

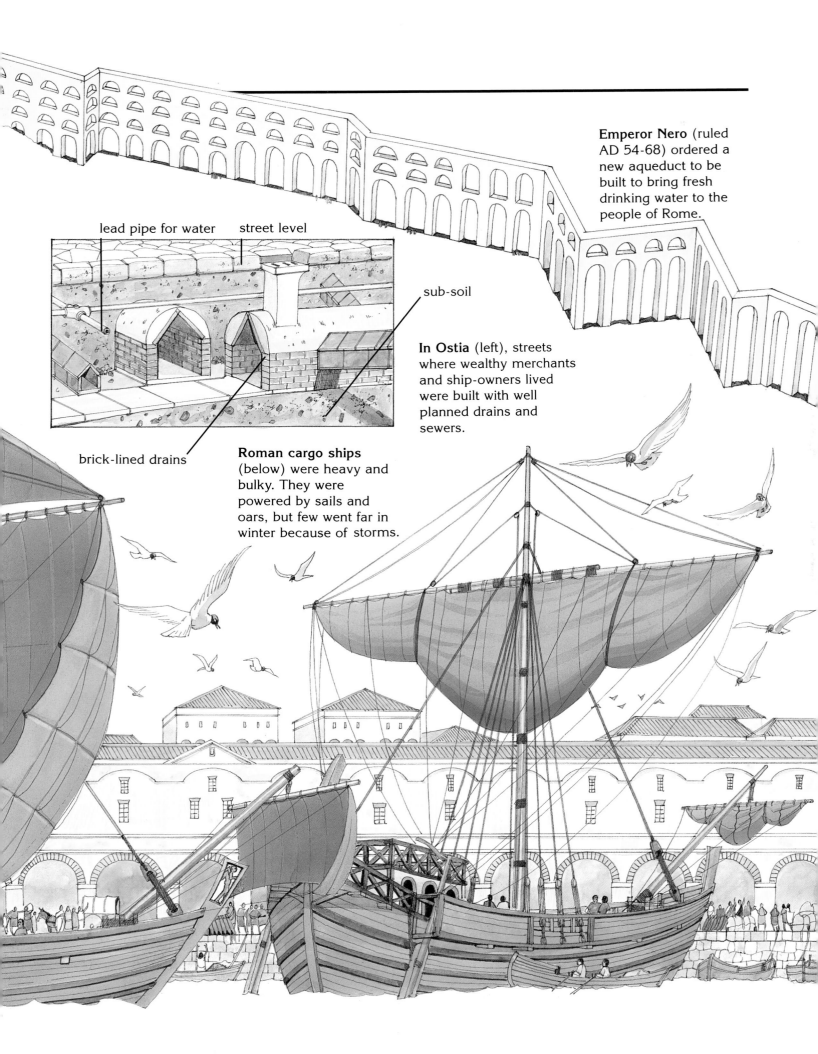

**Emperor Nero** (ruled AD 54-68) ordered a new aqueduct to be built to bring fresh drinking water to the people of Rome.

lead pipe for water    street level

sub-soil

**In Ostia** (left), streets where wealthy merchants and ship-owners lived were built with well planned drains and sewers.

brick-lined drains

**Roman cargo ships** (below) were heavy and bulky. They were powered by sails and oars, but few went far in winter because of storms.

# BREAD AND CIRCUSES

statue of Jupiter

plunder

**A triumphal procession**

**Victorious Roman** generals were honored with a triumphal

procession through the streets of Rome. Military standard-bearers led the way.

**Then came** statues of the gods. Jupiter, the Romans' principal god, came first.

**After the gods** came slaves carrying heaps of rich plunder from conquered lands.

Emperors and senators knew that if the Roman people went hungry they would riot. Angry mobs would rampage through the streets, looting and killing. To prevent this, the government provided free entertainments as well as free food.

Together, these 'gifts' were known as 'bread and circuses' – a 'circus' was an arena where chariot races were held – and they cost a vast amount. Money for food came from taxes, but entertainments were paid for by emperors or nobles from their own wealth.

There was an historic reason for this. In ancient Roman times, sports festivals had originally been staged in honor of the gods. Taking part in them, or even just watching, had been a religious act. Building a huge sports arena, like the Colosseum, had religious significance, too.

Human and animal sacrifices had also been part of ancient Roman religion. So staging fights between gladiators, or between men and animals, was a way of making a religious offering.

**Masks** worn by actors in tragic (left) and comic (right) plays.

**Roman playwrights** wrote about famous gods and heroes, myths and legends and every-day life. The bronze statue (right) shows a popular character in Roman plays – a cheeky slave.

**Men, women** and children all acted on the Roman stage. The Emperor Nero believed he had acting talent and liked taking part in plays.

**The second half** of the procession contained captured enemy chiefs, more prisoners and their weapons.

captive chieftains

**Lictors** (government officials) carried 'fasces', bundles of axes and sticks, as a sign of state power.

lictors

musicians    bulls for sacrifice    prisoners

**Musicians** followed, and behind them came priests leading animals for sacrifice to the gods.

**With this group** were men armed with special axes for killing the sacrificial animals.

**Enemy prisoners** bound in chains came next. They, too, were often killed.

**Behind** the prisoners marched soldiers blowing wild-sounding war-trumpets.

**Clay or bone tokens** (far left) were used like tickets. Small clay figures (near left) were made of the most popular actors.

**Chariot racing and races** by jockeys on horseback were very popular, and very dangerous, Roman spectator sports.

Rich Romans paid for sports and fights to mark important occasions in their lives, such as getting a top government job. They knew the entertainment was politically useful and hoped it would also please the gods.

**The victorious troops** marched at the rear.

**Senators and judges** followed the general.

# VESPASIAN'S PLANS

The Emperor Vespasian came to power in AD 69. He was a former soldier, brisk, energetic and efficient. He reformed the empire's administration, reorganized its finances and started to rebuild an area of Rome that had been damaged by a fire in AD 64. As part of his rebuilding scheme, he planned a huge public arena to be named after his family, the Flavians.

Vespasian's 'Flavian' arena (which we now call the Colosseum) was designed as a typical Roman amphitheater: a circular (or oval) arena with a central stage surrounded by rows of seats. It was similar to, but much larger than, the Theater of Marcellus, which had opened in Rome in AD 13.

**Coins** issued by the Emperor Vespasian (AD 69-79) and his son, the Emperor Titus (AD 79-81), builders of the Colosseum.

**Carving** from the Roman city of Trier (in present-day Germany) showing a tax collector seated at his counting-table, while a slave carries away a sack of money paid by conquered German tribes. Taxes like this helped pay for the Colosseum.

**Captured enemy** soldiers were forced to fight to the death in public open spaces to entertain Roman crowds. The captives were surrounded by a circle of well-armed soldiers to stop them running away.

**The earliest Roman** theaters had segment-shaped tiers of seats (left) made of strong wooden beams.

**Theater** at Epidaurus, Greece (left), built in the 3rd century BC. Roman architects often copied Greek designs.

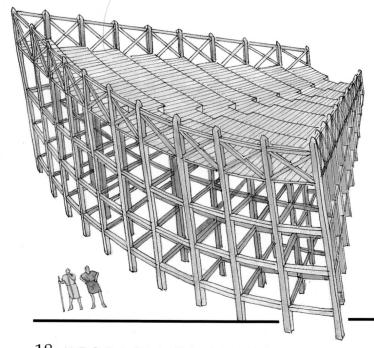

Amphitheaters developed from earlier Greek and Roman theaters built for performances of music and plays. Their design was also influenced by small, temporary arenas made out of wooden fences, where fights and plays were staged in the open air.

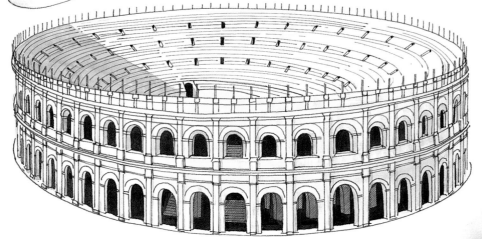

**Roman engineers** realized that a circular amphitheater could seat an audience twice the size of earlier, semicircular theaters and still give spectators a good view.

**Circular Roman** amphitheater (right) built at Nîmes, in southern France, 1st century AD.

**Circular amphitheaters** were used for all kinds of entertainment. Sometimes the floor was waterproofed with wood and canvas and flooded. Then mock sea-battles (left) were staged.

**Many buildings** in central Rome were destroyed by fire in AD 64. Vespasian took a motto 'Roma Resurgans' (Rome arising from the ashes) as the theme for his reign.

# PREPARING THE SITE

The Colosseum covered an area of about 6,000 square feet (about the size of a football field). It was surrounded by a wide pavement and cobbled streets. Roman engineers planned the building and its surroundings so that 50,000 spectators could come and go easily without getting crushed, panicking or causing a riot.

Their clever planning meant that an enormous area had to be cleared before building work could start. This was not an easy task. The site was next to the ruins of the Golden House, a splendid palace which had been built for Emperor Nero (AD 54-68), and which contained the marshy remains of a large lake, part of the beautiful gardens that had surrounded Nero's home. This had to be drained and stabilized with layers of hard-packed gravel and soil.

The Colosseum's builders left in place a massive statue, almost 130 feet high, of Nero. They would have been very surprised to learn that this statue would give their building a new name.

**Emperor Vespasian** was a good businessman too, carefully checking the plans and budgets for the Colosseum.

**Before** building work could start on the Colosseum, slaves had to level the ground and mark out the foundations, using a 'groma' (cross-sight) for accuracy. Roman architects and surveyors were very skilled. Many learned from the experience of Roman army surveyors, who built roads, forts and camps.

**Architect's** plan of the Colosseum (left).

**Nero's** colossal statue towered over the Colosseum building site and the ruins of his palace.

At first, the Colosseum was called the 'Flavian Amphitheater', as Vespasian had commanded. But before long it became known as the Colosseum, because of the 'colossal' statue of Nero that still stood nearby.

# ROMAN BUILDERS

Roman workers organized themselves into corporations or guilds, which tried to regulate wages and hours of work. They also maintained quality standards and gave emergency help to members in need.

There were guilds for the highly trained draftsmen and surveyors, as well as for the skilled building workers: masons, carpenters, iron-workers and demolition experts. There were also many ordinary laborers, transport workers and slaves.

Work started at the site in AD 72. The builders made such good progress that the arena was ready to be dedicated in AD 80, although work on the seating and decoration continued for another sixteen years.

Even with gangs of slaves to help the master craftsmen, building the Colosseum was a mammoth undertaking. Roman builders had no big machines, apart from hoists, to help them; all construction relied on muscle power.

**Roman** quarry workers cut huge blocks from the rock-face using simple technology. First they drilled grooves in the rock.

**Then** they hammered wooden wedges into the grooves and poured water on them. The wet wood swelled, splitting the rock into blocks.

**Finally** the blocks were trimmed to exact size and shape using sharp metal chisels and wooden mallets.

**Roman roads** were expertly made. First, a wide trench was dug. Then it was filled with layers of sand, rough stone blocks and pebbles mixed with gravel. It was finished with a layer of paving stones.

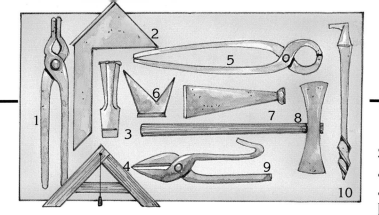

**Builders' tools:**
1. & 5. Pincers.
2. Square (for measuring right angles).
3. & 7. Chisels.
4. Plumb-line (to check walls were straight).

6. Trowel.
8. Mallet.
9. Cutters (used on metal).
10. Stone drill.

Stone was quarried about 20 miles away, then carried to Rome in ox-wagons along a specially built road. Bricks had to be fired and brought to the site, stone blocks had to be cut and carved to shape, massive wooden scaffolding had to be constructed and thousands of tons of concrete had to be mixed.

**A day in the life of a builder:**
**6 a.m.** (dawn) Gets up, puts on tunic and sandals.

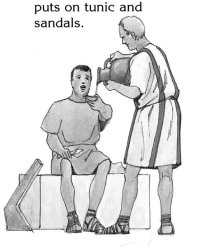

**11:30 a.m.** Lunch with workmates: bread, cheese, fruit, and water to drink.

**12 noon** Back at work, helping to haul blocks of stone to build the archway.

**6:30 a.m.** Has a simple breakfast of bread and water with his family.

**7 a.m.** Arrives at building site. Gets instructions for work from foreman.

**2 p.m.** Work is over for the day, so goes to the public baths with some friends.

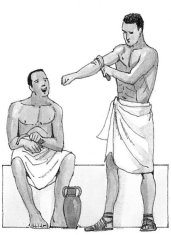

**10 a.m.** Busy helping to make a solid wooden scaffolding to support the next stone arch.

**5 p.m.** Buys ready-cooked food (meat pies and fig and honey cakes) to take home for dinner.

# LAYOUT AND MATERIALS

The layout of the Colosseum was simple: a high outer wall lined inside with sloping tiers of seats, with terraces and walkways in between. Below the rows of seats was a promenade, where spectators might walk and talk with their friends during the lunchtime interval between shows.

The architects and engineers who planned the Colosseum's layout also had to choose the most suitable building materials. It would have been impractical to make the entire building out of solid stone because it would soon have collapsed under its own weight. So they used tiers of strong, but much lighter, stone arches for the outer walls. The rest of the building was constructed around a framework of tall stone columns and the spaces in between the columns were filled in with cheaper, lighter materials.

Limestone blocks were used for this framework and to face the walls. They were carefully trimmed to shape, then fastened together with metal clamps. Several different types of material were used for 'filling in'. Tufa (a tough volcanic stone) was used for the lower walls and concrete (a Roman invention) and brick were used for the upper walls. The ceiling-vaults were made of pumice, a soft volcanic stone.

**Roman surveyors' tools:**
1. Bronze dividers, for measuring distances on architects' plans.
2. Folding foot-rule, marked off in inches.
3. Plumb-bob. This was a heavy lead weight on a string. It was used to check whether the walls were being built straight.

**Arches** were built over a wooden framework called a centering. It held the stone pillars at either side of the arch in place and stopped the wedge-shaped stones of the arch itself falling out while the arch was being built. Once the key-stone, the stone in the center of the arch, was in place, all the stones locked together and the centering could be removed.

**Walls** made of tiers of arches can be built several stories high. They are much stronger than walls made of solid stone.

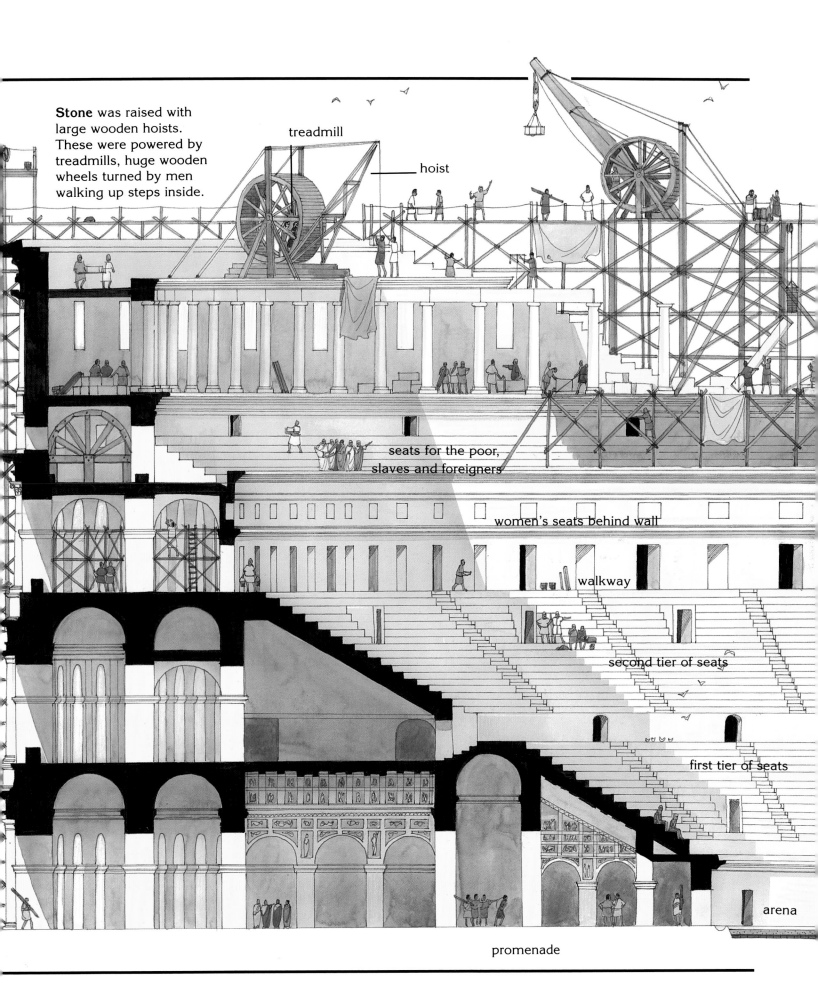

**Stone** was raised with large wooden hoists. These were powered by treadmills, huge wooden wheels turned by men walking up steps inside.

treadmill

hoist

seats for the poor, slaves and foreigners

women's seats behind wall

walkway

second tier of seats

first tier of seats

arena

promenade

# DECORATIONS

Emperor Vespasian died in AD 79. His sons Titus (AD 79-81) and Domitian (AD 81-96) became emperors after him. They, too, were successful soldiers, but not as good rulers as their father. Domitian was also an extremely cruel man.

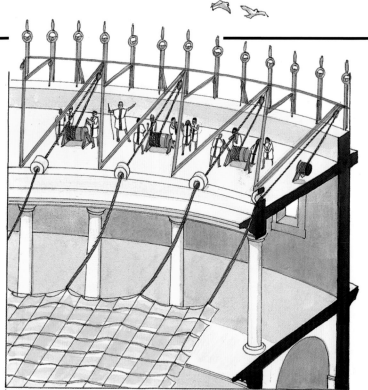

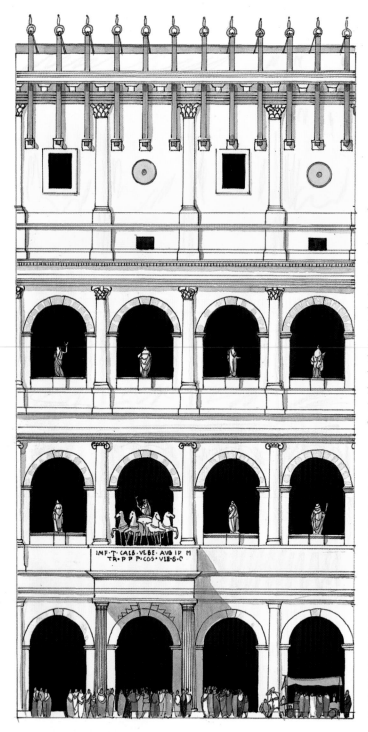

**The** huge seating area inside the Colosseum was far too big to be covered by a wooden roof. So canvas awnings, called 'velaria' (above), were made. They could be pulled across to shelter the spectators from rain or sun. They were operated by former sailors, who were used to handling big sails on Roman cargo ships.

**The walls** of the Colosseum (left) were decorated with carved stone columns. As was the custom, these columns were arranged in a set order: heavy 'Doric' columns on the ground, lighter 'Ionic' columns on the first floor and elaborate 'Corinthian' columns on the third floor. The top (fourth) floor columns were decorated with stone acanthus leaves.

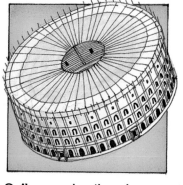

**Sailors** and sail-makers (top) working to install the canvas awnings. The Colosseum (above) with the canvas awning pulled across to shelter the spectators.

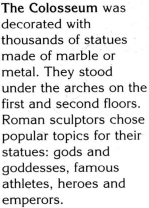

The **Colosseum** was decorated with thousands of statues made of marble or metal. They stood under the arches on the first and second floors. Roman sculptors chose popular topics for their statues: gods and goddesses, famous athletes, heroes and emperors.

**The** finished model was coated in wax, then covered in clay (right). Small pipes were stuck through the clay.

**Making a metal statue: The Romans** used the 'lost-wax' process to make metal statues. First, a full-size clay model was made (top).

**The** clay-covered statue was heated. The wax ran out (above) and molten metal was poured in (left) to replace it.

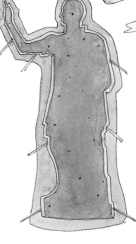

Both Titus and Domitian continued their father's great building project. Like him, they wanted to keep the citizens calm and happy, to honor the gods (including, now, their dead father) and to bring glory to the Flavian family name.

They decided that one of the best ways of doing this was by decorating the Colosseum with a large number of statues and by adorning the top of the outer wall with war shields. They hoped this would remind the people of their family's achievements in battle.

Roman sculptors were extremely skilled at producing lifelike portraits in metal, marble and stone. The central sculpture was a splendid portrait statue of Vespasian himself, driving the four-horse chariot that was reserved for the emperor. It was placed, with an inscription recording his decision to build the Colosseum, over the entrance which only emperors and their guests could use.

**When** the metal had cooled and hardened, the clay covering was chipped off (right) and the statue was complete.

# SEATS AND TICKETS

Entrance to the Colosseum was free. But that did not mean everyone could get in to watch the public executions, gladiator fights or wild-beast shows. Men from noble families, influential politicians and the emperor's friends were all allowed to sit in specially reserved seats. Among the rest of the population, only people who had been given tokens were allowed to enter and make their way along the well-planned walkways and corridors to their individually numbered seats.

There were different kinds of seats for the different classes of spectator. The emperor and his friends sat in a splendid marble enclosure beside the arena. There were private enclosures too, for the Vestal Virgins (temple priestesses), for male priests and for senior senators. The remaining seats were divided into three tiers: the first twenty rows were for wealthy citizens and the next sixteen rows were for men of middle rank. The third tier was for women only. Their seats were sheltered behind a high wall, so they could watch in privacy, away from the rude and noisy crowds.

Poor people, foreigners and slaves, who were rarely given tokens, stood high up on a wooden terrace at the back of the seats.

**The Colosseum** had seats for 45,000 people, plus room for 5,000 standing. Only citizens with entrance tokens (called 'tesserae') could get seats. Tokens and seats were numbered. This made it easier for spectators to find their places. Tokens were distributed by slaves belonging to the rulers, government officials and rich noblemen who sponsored the games, hoping to win popularity and keep the city calm. Spectators 'let off steam' by getting wildly excited at the Colosseum and were therefore much less likely to riot. Emperors planned their appearances at the Colosseum very carefully. They hoped to encourage displays of loyalty from the crowds.

wooden fence

outer walls decorated with statues

ordinary entrance

seats for the poor, slaves and foreigners

women's seats

second tier of seats

first tier of seats

arena

outside pavement

**The Colosseum** had 80 entrances: 76 were for the public, two were for the emperor and his friends and two were used by gladiators. The gladiators' marched into the arena through one of the entrances and their dead bodies were dragged out through the other.

emperor's entrance

MARK BERGIN MCMXCV

# BEHIND THE SCENES

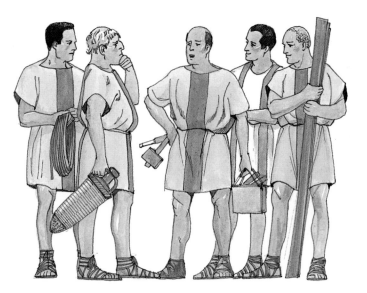

**The manager** (left) and his staff looked after day-to-day building maintenance and repairs.

**Workmen** (below) built strong barricades around the arena and kept the seats and walkways clean.

Running a huge building like the Colosseum required a large staff and hard-working managers to organize them. Some Colosseum staff could be seen by the spectators as they swept and cleaned, guarded the entrances and lugged heavy safety fences into place. But most people working at the Colosseum were less visible because they worked underground. While the gladiators fought and the lions roared overhead in the arena, dozens of workmen and slaves were busy in the maze of corridors, elevators, stairs and storerooms that lay hidden beneath the Colosseum, far away from public view.

**Grooms** (left) looked after the animals used for horse races, mock hunts and wild-beast shows.

**There** were amphi-theaters and gladiator fights in many Roman towns. In Pompeii, gladiators lived in the barracks (below). In Rome, gladiators lived in barracks (now destroyed) built by Emperor Claudius (AD 41-54).

**Roman** gladiators (left) were trained to fight by experienced instructors – usually ex-gladiators who had survived many fights.

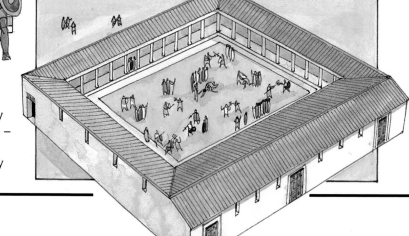

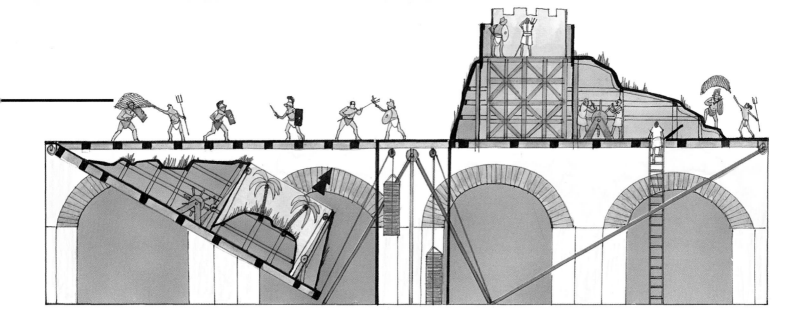

Some 'behind the scenes' tasks were quite pleasant: making stage-sets, painting replica boats for mock sea-fights or looking after the actors who staged early-morning comic shows. But most were not. Staff working underground had to guard frightened prisoners awaiting death, watch – and listen – as whole families of Christians were burned alive, or tease and torment wild animals in their cages until they were in a proper state of fury to 'perform'. At the end of the show, they had to dispose of the dead bodies and clean up all the blood.

**Many gladiator** fights and wild-beast shows were staged against a background of painted scenery, like a stage set. This was made by skilled craftsmen and hauled into position with pulleys and ropes.

**Notices** advertising gladiator fights were put on walls and trees by slaves of the rich men paying for the shows.

**Colosseum** staff (below left) collected seat tokens from spectators as they arrived.

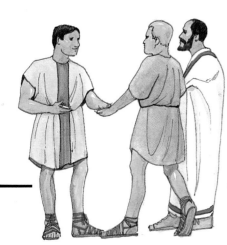

**Slaves** working for the Colosseum management had to remove the dead bodies.

**Specialist engineers** had to flood the arena when empeors wanted to stage mock sea-battles.

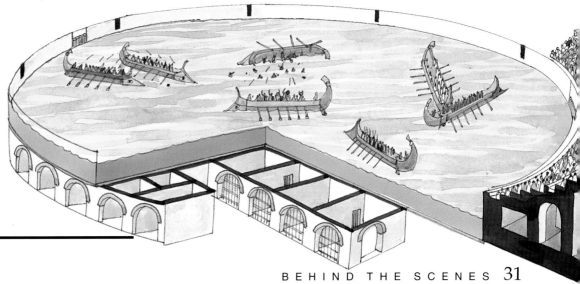

# WILD BEASTS

**Many wild animals**, like this antelope, suffered on the way to Rome.

**Mosaic** showing captive wild animals being taken to Rome.

**There** was an enormous demand for animals to be used in the Colosseum shows. All over the Roman empire huntsmen and soldiers hunted and captured all the wild beasts they could find.

Hunting was one of the Romans' most popular sports. But, of course, this was not possible in the city of Rome. So wild-beast shows were staged in amphitheaters like the Colosseum, where trapped animals, brought from hundreds of miles away, were let loose to be chased by gladiators or to fight captives and criminals. Sometimes, the sheer scale of death was horrifying. When Emperor Titus opened the Colosseum in AD 80, over five thousand animals were killed on the first day of the games.

Today, many people respect the natural environment and try to protect the creatures in it. But the Romans, like many other people in the past, had different views.

**Stone carving** (left) of gladiators fighting lions and bears.

**Mosaic** of a gladiator fighting against a wolf.

To the Romans nature was savage and had to be tamed. Wild beasts were wicked and stupid. They lacked the (supposedly) superior qualities of humans. So, the Romans said, it was fine to kill them for fun.

This attitude had terrible consequences. During the centuries when wild-beast shows were common (from 105 BC until AD 532), several species became extinct in Roman lands. Hippopotami died out in Egypt, lions were exterminated in the Middle East and no elephants were left in North Africa. Today many people would say that watching such mindless killing harmed the spectators, too.

**Wild animals** were kept in cages under the arena, then brought up in a special elevator. When the cage was opened, they were set free to face the gladiators in the arena.

**Rhinos**, elephants and ostriches were captured in Africa and brought to Rome.

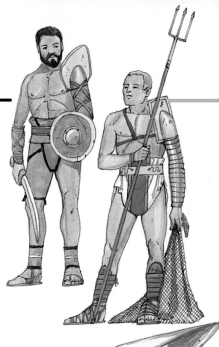

**Thracian** gladiator (right) armed with a short sword and small shield. The gladiator (far right) is called a 'retiarius' and armed only with a trident and a net.

**Magnificent** helmet, decorated with little statues and feathers, worn by a successful gladiator, plus his short sword.

# GLADIATORS

Gladiators were the superstars of Roman public games. Although a few achieved fame and riches, on average, half the gladiators involved in any particular fight were likely to be killed.

Who became gladiators? Some men had no choice. Trainers bought them at the slave-market because they looked strong and fit for fighting. The trainers took them home or to rented barracks, fed them, housed them and trained them in combat skills. But they never let them go. These slave-gladiators were kept locked up like prisoners and had to fight at their trainer's command. Trainers hired out teams of gladiators to rich men wanting to put on a show. They made a lot of money.

**Charioteer** (right) wearing a helmet, tunic and riding boots. He carries a horse-whip. A fully-armed gladiator (far right), known as a 'Samnite', after a war-like tribe that once lived near Rome, or a 'secutor', because he cut off men's lives.

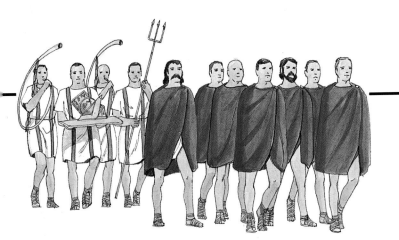

**Gladiators** marched into the arena wearing cloaks of purple – the emperor's color. They were accompanied by musicians blowing war-trumpets.

**They** circled the arena, then stopped before the emperor's box and bowed to him, saying, 'Hail, Emperor. We who are about to die salute you.'

**Each** Colosseum show usually started in the morning with cruel comic duels fought by women or people with physical disabilities.

**Defeated** gladiators (left) raised a finger of the left hand, to show they were begging the emperor for mercy. If he gave the thumbs-up signal they lived.

**Gladiators** were often mismatched. Romans enjoyed seeing men fighting desperately.

**If the emperor** turned his thumb downwards, they were killed by a slave dressed as Pluto, the god of the underworld (above). He hit them on the forehead with a wooden hammer.

Some poor young men joined a trainer's team because it seemed the only alternative to starvation. They thought it worth risking their lives for a few months of good food, plus the faint chance of glory. Other volunteers included rich, daredevil young men addicted to the thrills and violence. Perhaps they were rather like racing-drivers today, though the risks they faced were far greater.

A few women, seeking dangerous excitements, tried to train as gladiators, too. But they were banned from the Colosseum and all other sports arenas in AD 200.

**Victorious** gladiators (above) were given rich prizes and allowed to hang their weapons in the Temple of Hercules.

**Top gladiators** (left) attracted many fans, especially rich women.

# FEASTS AND FEARS

The Colosseum has been called 'a torture-chamber and a human-slaughterhouse.' No wonder many gladiators facing a fight and captives and convicts awaiting execution spent their last night in misery and despair.

On the evening before a fight the emperor or noble paying for the games would arrange a lavish feast and invite all the gladiators to share the meal together. Some gladiators ate little, so they would be alert for the fight next day. Others ate greedily, knowing it might be their last meal.

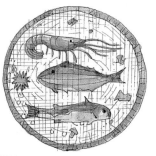

**Roman mosaic** of the ingredients for a rich seafood meal. Gladiators feasted on luxury foods at public banquets the night before a big fight in the Colosseum.

**Successful** gladiators often became very rich. But they knew they would not live long. They dictated their wills to professional scribes.

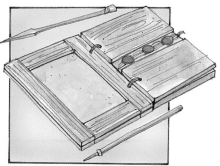

**The Roman** men and women who dined with gladiators before a fight enjoyed the knowledge that many of their fellow diners might be dead the next day.

**Roman scribes** wrote with quill pens on parchment, or used wax-tablets and styluses like these.

**Music** was a more pleasant and peaceful form of entertainment. Popular Roman instruments included:
1. Sistrum.  2. Pipe.
3. Double flute.
4. Castanets.
5. Trumpet.
6. Panpipes.

**Many Roman** games were much less blood-thirsty than gladiator fights. Gambling with dice and throwing knucklebones were both very popular.

**Carved** ivory game counter (top) showing girl with double flute.

**Mosaic** (above) showing double flute player and dancing girl.

Members of the public were invited to watch this unpleasant feast and, occasionally, to join in. The brave, brutal gladiators fascinated many Roman citizens, including noblewomen and emperors' wives. They watched all their heroes' battles, cheering them as they entered the Colosseum on the day of the fight. Emperor Commodus (AD 180-192) was said to be the son of a famous gladiator, with whom his mother had had a secret love affair. Certainly, Commodus enjoyed fighting at the Colosseum. He was assassinated there, while dressed in gladiator's clothes.

**Before** a fight, gladiators were driven to the Colosseum in carts, then they formed themselves into a procession to make a dramatic entrance. Well-wishers dropped gifts of flowers to their favorite gladiators as they entered the Colosseum.

# THE BIG FIGHT

A particularly large fight between gladiators was called a 'hoplomachia'. After the gladiators had paraded around the arena, their weapons were checked and the battle-order was announced. Duels might be arranged according to a master-plan for the day's entertainment, or chosen simply by lot. The Colosseum orchestra – flutes, trumpets, horns and an organ – played a fanfare and the fighting began. The gladiators slashed and stabbed savagely – a hesitant fighter would not last long. Trainers stood beside the arena, urging their best gladiators on to fresh victories.

Gladiators who managed to survive several fights might be offered the 'rudis' by the emperor.  This was a wooden sword and it meant that the gladiator could stop fighting. He could sell the silver trophies and gold medals he had won as prizes and retire.

Astonishingly, some of the most successful gladiators who had been offered the 'rudis' gave it back, negotiated new contracts with their trainers and continued fighting. Perhaps they felt life was not worth living without the excitement, the shining armor, the thrill of battle, the smell of blood in the arena and the roar of the bloodthirsty crowd.

**On the far side** of the arena, a musician sounds a fanfare as the judge of the gladiators' fights proclaims a winner.

**Armor** worn by gladiators:
1. Helmet to protect the face of a gladiator pitted against one armed with a trident.
2. Metal shin protector fastened around the leg with leather straps.
3. Protective metal plate worn on a gladiator's left shoulder.
4. Metal guard worn on the right wrist.
5. Elaborately decorated metal shin guard. Armor like this was extremely expensive and was usually part of the prize given to victorious gladiators.
6. Bronze helmet worn by a hoplomachus, a very heavily armed gladiator.

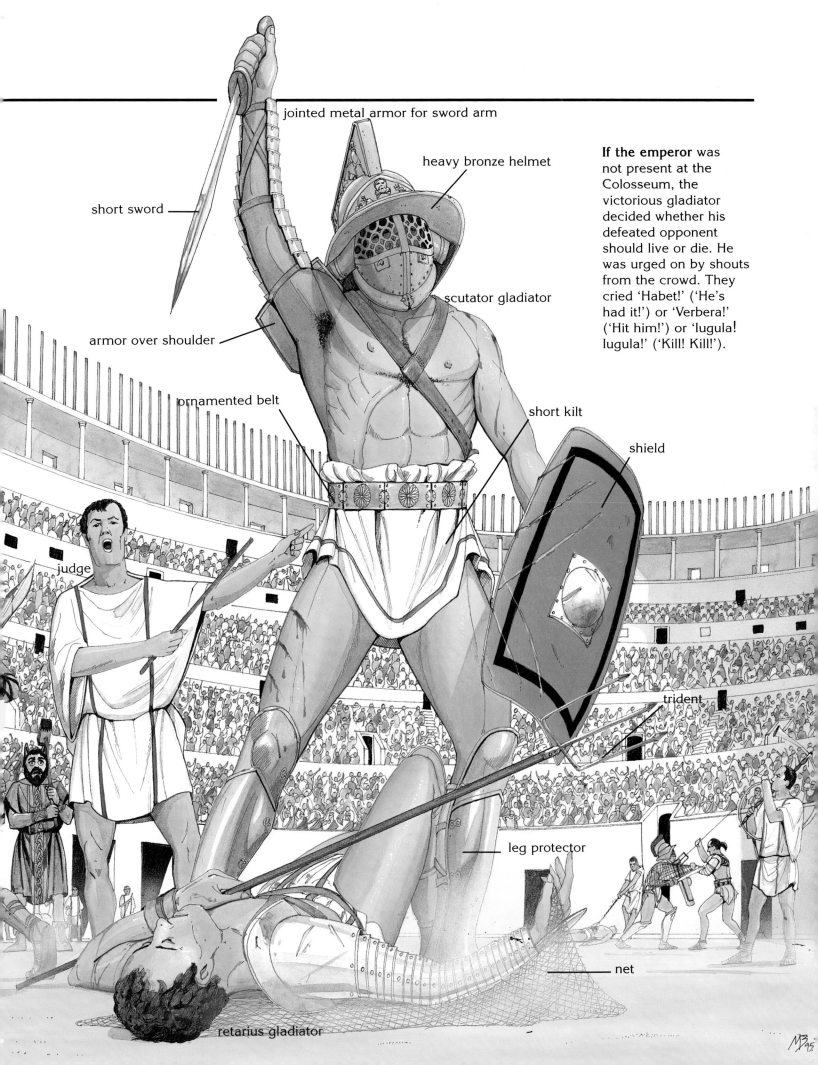

jointed metal armor for sword arm

heavy bronze helmet

short sword

scutator gladiator

armor over shoulder

If the emperor was not present at the Colosseum, the victorious gladiator decided whether his defeated opponent should live or die. He was urged on by shouts from the crowd. They cried 'Habet!' ('He's had it!') or 'Verbera!' ('Hit him!') or 'Iugula! Iugula!' ('Kill! Kill!').

ornamented belt

short kilt

shield

judge

trident

leg protector

net

retarius gladiator

# MARTYRS AND SLAVES

Thousands of convicted criminals were killed in the Colosseum. Roman emperors thought that Christians were criminals too, because they would not worship the Roman gods. So many Christians were executed as enemies of the state, in various appalling ways.

The first Christian to be martyred (killed because of his faith) in the Colosseum was Ignatius of Antioch, in around AD 110. Later, when Christian rulers came to power in Rome, Ignatius was honored as a saint.

Like ordinary criminals, Christians were often killed by hungry leopards or lions. A cruel story told how this idea for execution originated: a wooden lift containing a criminal accidentally broke, dropping him among beasts in the arena. The watching

**In 73 BC**, a captive called Spartacus who was being forced to train as a gladiator, led a gladiators' revolt. Armed only with knives,

Spartacus and his friends fought their way out of the gladiators' school and took refuge in the mountains. Many runaway slaves joined them and they became a formidable army. It was two years before they were defeated. Spartacus died in battle, but the Romans crucified 6,000 of his comrades beside the Appian Way.

crowd thought this was such a good joke that 'throwing people to the lions' became a popular part of the Colosseum shows.

One Christian martyr, St Telemachus, died bravely (around AD 404) in a very different way. He was outraged at the sight of slaves and prisoners being forced to fight until they died. He leapt into the arena and tried to part the fighting men. He was put to death for disrupting the games, but, soon, other people began to share his horror at the brutality of the Colosseum shows.

**The Appian Way** was the main road from Rome. It ran for 100 miles to the city of Capua. After Spartacus's revolt, there was a crucified man every 100 feet or so for the road's entire length.

**Christians** and criminals were tied to wooden frames, then wheeled into the arena to be mauled by lions (left). Spectators were protected by an iron fence built around the edge of the arena to stop the lions escaping. Mosaic (below) showing a Christian being killed by a leopard.

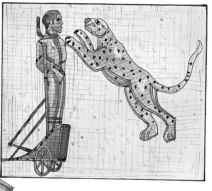

# LATER CENTURIES

The last gladiator fight was held in the Colosseum in AD 404. After that fights were banned on the orders of Emperor Honorius (AD 395-423). He was a Christian, and believed that many old Roman customs were sinful, including human sacrifices and the Colosseum's gladiatorial games. But the bloody wild-beast shows in front of cheering audiences continued for at least another hundred years.

Over the centuries, the Colosseum became neglected. It was damaged by earthquakes, the statues were stolen and tons of its stones were taken for new buildings.

In 1855, British botanist Richard Deakin published a book entitled *Flora of the Colosseum*. In it, he listed 420 different varieties of plant he had found growing wild on the neglected site, including:
1. Christ's thorn.
2. Anemone.
3. Asphodel.

visitors to the Colosseum c.1780

**In the** 18th and 19th centuries, wealthy young noblemen went on a 'Grand Tour' of historic sites in Europe to complete their education. They were all very impressed by the Colosseum, even though it was half-ruined. One of the best descriptions of it was written in 1805 by the Frenchman the Vicomte de Chateaubriand.

**In 1744**, Pope Benedict XIV gave orders for a huge wooden cross to be placed in the center of the Colosseum as a memorial to all the Christians who had been martyred there. He dedicated the whole building as a holy shrine and gave orders for a monk to preach a sermon in front of the memorial cross every Friday.

It was used as a fortress, for plays and concerts (although the acoustics were terrible), for bullfights and even as stables for horses and cows. After around 1650, it was visited by wealthy tourists from many lands, eager to study Roman remains. Among them were the English poets Byron and Shelley, the German author Goethe and the French painter Corot.

The first serious attempts to preserve the Colosseum's structure were not made until the mid 19th century. Today, although the stonework has been carefully repaired, the Colosseum, like many ancient buildings, faces a new threat: air pollution.

# Colosseum Chronology

All dates AD

| | |
|---|---|
| **72** | Colosseum building work begins. |
| **80** | Emperor Titus leads dedication ceremony. First gladiatorial games at the Colosseum. |
| **96** | Colosseum completed. |
| **c.110** | St Ignatius of Antioch is first known Christian martyr to be killed in the Colosseum. |
| **180-192** | Emperor Commodus takes part in over 300 gladiatorial fights; is assassinated at the Colosseum. |
| **200** | Women gladiators banned from Colosseum. |
| **247-248** | Emperor Philip the Arab stages huge festival in the Colosseum to mark the thousandth anniversary of the founding of Rome. |
| **253** | Four Christian martyrs burned alive just outside the Colosseum. |
| **320** | The Colosseum is struck by lightning; remarkably unharmed. |
| **399** | Emperor Honorius bans gladiator training schools. |
| **401** | Captive Saxons, forced to fight as gladiators, strangle each other in the cells under the Colosseum rather than face a shameful death in front of Roman crowds. |
| **c.404** | Christian monk Telemachus leaps into the Colosseum arena to try to stop fights. He is executed. |
| **404** | Emperor Honorius abolishes pagan gladiatorial games. |
| **410** | Visigoth invaders attack Rome; but do not damage Colosseum. |
| **422** | Earthquake damages Colosseum; repaired 467 and 472. |
| **508** | Further earthquake damage. |

523     Last wild-beast show in Colosseum.

c.590   Colosseum arena overgrown by grass.

604     Grass growing on Colosseum walls.

735     The Venerable Bede, a Christian monk, is first to record the name 'Colosseum' in writing.

800     Christian pilgrims start to travel to Rome; admire remains of Colosseum.

847     Further earthquake damage.

1084    Normans invade Rome; devastate area around the Colosseum.

1144    Colosseum turned into a fortress by noble family, the Frangipani. Houses, taverns, workshops built nearby.

1150    Colosseum (wrongly) described as 'Temple of the Sun' in guidebook *The Marvels of Rome*, written by a Christian monk.

1231    More earthquake damage.

1320    Colosseum clearly shown in first-known medieval drawing of the city of Rome.

1322    Colosseum used to stage bullfights.

1337    The Italian poet Petrarch visits Colosseum.

1349    Further earthquake damage.

1381    Italian religious guilds use Colosseum to stage mystery (religious-story) plays.

1400    Colosseum stone used for new buildings in Rome.

1431    Renaissance scholar Bacciolni laments that Colosseum 'is already half destroyed'.

1451    Over 2,000 cartloads of stone removed from Colosseum on orders of Pope Nicholas I for new buildings.

1490s    Passion plays performed in Colosseum at Easter, re-enacting the death of Jesus Christ.

1535    Black-magic rituals in Colosseum at night.

c.1550    Renaissance artists visit Colosseum to study details of Roman design.

1675    Colosseum now a store for chemicals used to make gunpowder.

1703    Further earthquake damage.

1744    Pope Benedict XIV erects memorial cross to Christians martyred in Colosseum. Arranges weekly sermon to be preached there.

1750s    Colosseum now surrounded by wild grassland, called the 'Cow Pasture'. Used as stable for horses and cows.

c.1750    Many tourists visit Rome and admire Colosseum. Local people comment 'If the Colosseum could be picked up, tourists would carry it away.'

c.1750-c.1800    Poets, painters, philosphers and historians from all over Europe visit the Colosseum.

1812    French military architects clear away plants growing on Colosseum walls.

1817    British poet, Lord Byron, writes about Colosseum: 'Heroes have trod this spot, 'tis on their dust ye tread.'

1825    Pope Leo XII builds buttresses to support Colosseum walls.

1844    English novelist Charles Dickens calls Colosseum 'the ghost of old Rome – a wicked, wonderful old city.'

1850s    Pope Pius IX organizes repairs to Colosseum.

1855    Deakin's *Flora of the Colosseum* published.

1878    American novelist Henry James writes short story *Daisy Miller*. Daisy, a young tourist, goes to view romantic Colosseum ruins by moonlight, catches fever from its 'villainous miasma' and dies.

1890s    Area around Colosseum cleared of other buildings.

1912    Irish playwright George Bernard Shaw writes play *Androcles and the Lion* about a Christian captive who helps a timid lion in the Colosseum. They become friends and escape to freedom.

1951    Grand concert held to celebrate the fiftieth anniversary of Italian composer Giuseppe Verdi's death, but not a musical success, since the Colosseum's acoustics are bad.

1996    One thousand, nine hundred years since Colosseum building works completed.

# GLOSSARY

**Amphitheater**, circular or oval-shaped building, consisting of an open central arena, surrounded by rows of seats.

**Aqueduct**, raised channel built to carry fresh water.

**Arena**, (1) the central open space of an amphitheater. (2) a building used for sports contests or army displays, usually roofless.

**Barracks**, large building where soldiers eat and sleep.

**Circus**, a long arena with curved ends, where chariot races and horse races were held.

**Emperor**, the ruler of an empire. Usually had tremendous personal power.

**Empire**, lands ruled by a stronger power.

**Forum**, large market-place in the middle of Rome and other Roman towns. Important as a meeting place, as well as for trading.

**Games**, word used to describe a variety of sporting events, including gladiator fights. Games had originally been staged in honor of the gods.

**Gladiators**, professional fighters who took part in battles arranged for public entertainment in Rome. Many of those who survived became popular heroes and won rich prizes.

**Guild**, organization of workers which aimed to provide training, control quality, fix wages and offer welfare help.

**Imperial**, belonging to an empire.

**Insula**, the Roman word for a block of flats.

**Litter**, a form of transport. A lightweight, portable bed carried shoulder-high by slaves.

**Martyrs**, people who are killed because of their religious beliefs.

**Papyrus**, paper made from reeds that grew in the River Nile, in Egypt.

**Patricians**, the noble families of Rome.

**Princeps**, the Roman emperor's title. It means 'first' (among citizens with equal rights).

**Pumice**, lightweight stone, formed from cooled volcanic lava.

**Republic**, a system of government in which the leaders are elected by the people. Republics do not have ruling families which hand on power from parents to children.

**Rudis**, a wooden sword offered to a victorious gladiator by the emperor as a sign that he was free to retire.

**Senate**, an assembly of respected men who had held top government posts. They offered advice to government leaders and could suggest new laws.

**Senator**, a member of the Senate.

**Tufa**, a grey stone, formed from layers of compressed volcanic dust.

**Velaria**, canvas awnings providing a roof to shelter spectators in the Colosseum.

**Vestal Virgins**, priestesses from noble families who guarded the 'sacred flame' in a temple in the middle of Rome.

# INDEX